CATS

A PORTRAIT OF THE ANIMAL WORLD

Marcus Schneck & Jill Caravan

TODTRI

This book was designed and produced by
Todtri Productions Limited
P.O. Box 20058
New York, NY 10023-1482
Fax: (212) 279-1241

Printed and bound in Singapore

ISBN 1-880908-18-2

Authors: Marcus Schneck & Jill Caravan

Producer: Robert M. Tod
Book Designer: Mark Weinberg
Editor: Mary Forsell
Photo Editor: Natasha Milne
Design Associate: Jackie Skroczky
Typesetting: Command-O, NYC

INTRODUCTION

When a cat raises its head directly, it is attempting to convey dominance. The animal's pricked ears convey interest in its surroundings.

The domestic cat, the house cat, the show cat—we see them everywhere, every day. Very few places on earth can we go where we won't find the cat. Only a few places can we venture where the cat is not a common and beloved member of the household.

The cat has been close to man for at least 4,500 years. That's how far back the earliest physical evidence—some distinctive cat images on the walls of Egyptian tombs, carved feline statues, and mummified cat bodies—has been dated.

Those first 'domestic' cats came to live in close proximity to man of their own free will. They were African wild cats (Felis lybica), which still exist as a wild species today, that chose to move into the alleys and shadows of man's towns and cities. There they found abundant prey in the rats and mice that were rampant in man's grain storage bins.

For generations before that first connection was made, ancient Egyptian religion had encompassed many references to catlike figures and gods taking on the form of cats. The lion had been used for those parts of the ceremonies where a living embodiment of the cat was needed. But the 'king of beasts' was also a beastly handful for the priests to control and mas-

ter. This new, smaller cat that was turning up in ever greater numbers presented a perfect alternative. Very shortly after the African wild cats began frequenting the granaries, some of its numbers were showing up in religious ceremonies.

And those numbers were most definitely on the increase. Given its new protected status and the abundance of its prey, the population of semi-tame African wild cats skyrocketed. Although the religious significance and absolutely protected status stayed with the cats, now there were enough of them that some found their ways into households outside the temples. The first generation of the true domestic cat had been developed.

The Egyptians held their cats in such high esteem—even to the extent of having them mummified and buried with them in their tombs—that the spread of the animals was restrained for many years. The Greeks, active trading partners of the Egyptians, noted the mousing abilities of the cat, offered much in trade for a few, and eventually resorted to stealing several pairs. In turn, the offspring that those cats produced in profusion eventually were traded with other trading partners of the

Greeks; Romans, Gauls, and Celts. Thus, the domestic cat had begun its spread throughout Europe.

Although this is the most widely accepted explanation of the origins of our domestic cat, there are those that believe the European wild cat also contributed some individuals to the initial domestication movement in the more northerly climes. The process would have been much the same as that which took place in northern Africa.

The first domestic cats, other than some limited numbers of big cats that were held in captivity by some ancient South American cultures, came to the New World on the far side of the Atlantic with the first European settlers. No record has been verified as to when the first domestic cat set foot on American soil, where it came from, or what breed it may have been. However, it's a relatively safe bet that some ship's cat or settler's farm cat captured that honour very early in the European settlement of the Americas.

That's how the domestic cat came to be one of the most widespread animal species on earth, but it's only the past few thousand years of the cat's history. The first chapters of the story extend back millions more years.

CAT HISTORY

The domestic cat is part of that segment of the animal kingdom we know as mammals, the same group that includes man and dog and about fifteen thousand other species. It's a very small group when compared to the few million total species that still exist today, but it's also the most evolutionarily advanced group. Females in this class of animals have milk-producing mammae, and both sexes of all species within the group have hair and bodies that regulate their own internal temperatures.

Mammals also are a relatively recent development on the evolutionary timeline. The first mammals evolved from reptiles more than two hundred million years ago.

They started their climb to the dominant form of life on earth about seventy million years ago.

Within the overall class of mammals, one subgroup is made up of the carnivores, the meat eaters. Even within the relatively small class known as mammals, the carnivores make up only a small grouping. The first carnivores that we have fossil evidence of were the Miacis, small weasel-like creatures. Following the irresistible pull of evolution, the Miacis eventually developed along several different lines to fill the various niches that were available to them. From forty-five to fifty million years ago these paths brought them to the dawning of the carnivores that still exist today, including the cats.

The ears, muzzle, legs, feet, and tail of a cat are known as the animal's points in show circles. When these points carry a different colour from the rest of the body, the animal is referred to as a colourpoint, in this case a colourpoint Persian.

The sabre-toothed tiger was one of the experiments in evolution that found its niche for a period of time but then became extinct. The ancestors of our domestic cat obviously fared better.

Only a very few breeds of cat should never have any outdoor time, and many actually relish or even need such activity.

However, evolution was still a long way from finished with its work on these animals. As those early cats spread out across the planet, to exploit new niches as they emerged, the cats continued their development into new creatures better equipped for survival.

Some of nature's experiments in new adaptations didn't work out, or the niches for which they had developed disappeared, and these were discarded along the way. We know this action as extinction. The most widely recognised cat species that followed this route into oblivion was the sabre-toothed tiger, the last of which was alive as recently as thirteen thousand years ago. Many more species met with this fate than were able to survive through to today.

The ancestors of our domestic cats were among the survivor species. Although they existed at the same time as the sabre-toothed tiger and similarly now-departed species, these smaller creatures were somehow better adapted to continue on. The earliest fossils that closely resemble today's cats have been dated at about twelve million years ago.

Actually only three groups of cats of the

The lion and cheetah represent two of the three genera of cats that still exist today: <u>Panthera</u> and <u>Acinonyx</u>, respectively. Our domestic cat represents the third, <u>Felis</u>, or small cats.

9

Two young cheetahs display the short muzzles, whiskers, and large eyes for which the family Felidae is known. Both cheetahs and lions live in prides, but most cats are solitary.

many that existed around that time made it to today. These groups are known as genera. The domestic cat is part of the genus *Felis*, which is made up of the smaller cats with a rigid hyoid bone at the base of their tongues that prevents them from roaring. Lions and tigers, the big cats, are in the genus *Panthera*. Their hyoid bones move freely, allowing them to roar. And the third genus, *Acinonyx*, contains only one species, the cheetah.

Within those genera are about forty species of cat that still exist today. Our domestic cat is just one of these, although man's intervention has helped it to become the most diverse and widespread.

Within all this biology, natural history, and history, the critical point to remember in this tale of how the cat came into domestication is this: The cat made the initial decision to come into close contact with man. With all of our other domesticated animals, such as the dog, the horse and the cow, it was man who originally decided that those animals offered qualities that he could benefit from if they were 'tamed'.

CAT LORE

Such an extraordinary beginning probably is at least part of the root of the many mysteries and near-mysticism that still surround our cats. While nearly everything they do can be clearly explained in terms of the animals that the cats are, complete with animal senses and animal instincts, legend and lore abound about this animal.

A sixth sense, some sort of awareness on a plane that we humans can only imagine, is often cited as the explanation for the cat's apparent ability to predict things to come. They've been known to flee buildings before an earthquake rocks the area. Or, on a more mundane level, some cats have built impressive reputations as prognosticators of coming storms. In both instances it is the extraordinary sense of hearing that the cat possesses as a predator of the first order that accounts for the feats, rather than some magical powers.

Contributing to the mystical atmosphere that seems to be affixed to the cat for eternity is the animal's refusal to become fully a servant of man, a role that our dogs have accepted eagerly. Our cats remain very much their own animals, giving in to our commands and wishes only when they suit their purposes as well.

Most cat fanciers trace the origins of the domestic cat back to the African wild cat, but there is strong evidence that the European wild cat (shown here) also brought itself into domestication and led to a number of our breeds today.

Today these special qualities endear the cat to man—actually it's more of an all-or-nothing, love 'em or hate 'em affair for most of us—but it has not always been like this. In the Middle Ages, when nearly every unfortunate happenstance was blamed on this or that action of a witch, the cat became linked as an ally or familiar of witches. Everything the animal did or was capable of doing, from being able to see well at night to landing on its feet when dropped, was cited as further evidence of the connection. Like the poor humans who were accused of black magic, the cat was persecuted throughout Europe by representatives of the Christian church. The fact that the ani-mal was revered in some other religions like those of ancient Egypt didn't help the cat's plight.

It was not uncommon for cats to be cruci-fied and burned at the stake. By about the year 1400 the cat was nearly extinct throughout Europe. It's ironic that the most effective deterrent to vermin was being destroyed just as huge populations of rats were spreading the plague across the Continent.

As the fear of witchcraft-caused physical and mental abnormalities finally subsided, so did the persecution of the cat. A stroll along nearly any European street today will reveal just how well the animal has rebounded.

The Abyssinian breed was nearly wiped out three times in this century: During both world wars, when food supplies ran short, and then in the 1960s, when feline leukemia struck.

The Manx is a naturally occurring breed, com-pletely lacking any tail whatsoever, which gives the animal a stumpy, squatting appearance.

ONE SPECIES, MANY BREEDS

When we use the general term cat or domestic cat we are covering a full complement of one hundred or so breeds that are officially recognised by one or more of the national and international cat organisations. It is a common misconception outside the ranks of the cat fanciers that each breed represents a distinct species. This is incorrect. The domestic cat is a single species, whether the individual animal is a long-haired Persian or a nearly hairless Sphynx. The many new breeds that have been developed in recent years, and will be developed over the next few years thanks to our quickly growing knowledge of genetics, are and will be members of that same single species, *Felis domesticus*.

Each breed can generally be placed within one of five broad categories: Persians, other longhairs, British shorthairs, American shorthairs, and Oriental shorthairs. However, some of the most recent breeds are so new that full standards for what represents the best qualities of the breed have not been developed and exact classification is not yet possible. Others remain very controversial with the same results.

Controversy sometimes enters into the classification and official recognition of some breeds because of the unique qualities that make the breed unique. For example, the Peke-Face Persian is a snub-nosed mutation that occurs naturally among litters of the red Persian and red tabby Persian breeds. Because the build of the snout and muzzle can lead to respiratory and eating problems,

The Persian breed is the most popular purebreed today throughout most major cat organisations. It also is one of the oldest recognised breeds, represented among the cats shown in the very first cat show in 1598.

The seal-point Birman carries the colours and markings that most closely resemble those described in a legend of how the cat came to be. The legend holds that the cat originated in the death of a Buddhist priest.

The Cornish rex first appeared in one red-and-white male born into a litter in Cornwall, Great Britain, in 1950. It was the sole mutation among a litter of otherwise normal farm kittens.

All colours and patterns are recognised by most cat organisations in the Cornish rex breed.

The Siamese is to the Far East what the Persian and the British shorthair are to the West. It was the original breed throughout much of the Far East, a common pet around royal courts as early as the sixteenth century.

the Peke-Face is not recognised by organisations in Great Britain.

The principal organisations today are the Governing Council of the Cat Fancy in Great Britain, the oldest such organisation, founded in 1910; the Cat Fanciers' Association, the largest organisation in the United States; the American Cat Association, the oldest cat fancier organisation in the United States; Cat Fanciers' Federation; Crown Cat Fanciers' Federation; United Cat Federation; International Cat Association; Canadian Cat Association; and Federation Internationale Feline de L'Europe. With so many organisations, each with its own set of standards and preferences—and these are only the major organisations—is it any wonder that disagreements arise on a regular basis?

All this started in the mid to late nineteenth century in Europe, most notably in Great Britain. For thousands of years prior to that time, the cat was primarily a functional animal, whose purpose was to keep down the home's or farm's rodent population. But, in the mid-1800s, owners began

The Devon rex has the unique habit among cats of wagging its tail when contented but excited, similar to the actions of a dog. Its curly coat inspired the nickname of 'poodle cat'.

The true origins and development of the Russian blue are clouded by the various names under which it has travelled. At various times prior to the 1940s, it also was known as the Archangel blue, Maltese, and Spanish blue.

The first Russian blue specimens to leave their country of origin were cats that found their way to Great Britain aboard Russian ships in the late 1800s.

to take special interest in the particular characteristics that defined their favourite cats. Attempts to breed the animals to bring out and build upon those characteristics began in earnest. The first full-fledged cat show was held in 1871 in London's Crystal Palace, with twenty-five different judging classes. With a certain national pride, most early breeding attempts concentrated on those breeds considered to be 'native' to the British Isles. As a result, these were also the most widely shown breeds in early competitions.

However, it was a matter of only a few years until other breeds were being brought back and bred by members of the cat fancy who had encountered them in their travels. The Persian, the most popular breed today, was the first such introduction, followed shortly thereafter by the Siamese.

A primary function of the many different organisations is to develop and maintain standards of the pedigree. These standards represent the ideal characteristics that all breeders should strive for within a specific

Although the Russian blue originated in the cold climate of Archangel in Russia, the breed today tends to prefer warmer temperatures and will seek out these spots in the home.

The Scottish fold is one of our more recent breeds, emerging from a few kittens born with folded ears on a Scottish farm in 1961.

British cat organisations do not officially recognise the Scottish fold as a breed because of the potential hearing problems that the folded ears might contribute.

With its folded ears and broad eyes, the Scottish fold can have a somewhat sad look to it, however it's actually a very playful and hearty breed.

The true standard of the ocicat includes a spotted pattern that resembles the wild ocelot, for which the breed is named.

Even when breeding very pure Scottish fold parents, some of the kittens often do not carry the folded ear trait.

The snowshoe is a recent breed that was developed through the crossing of bicolour American shorthairs and Siamese. Show standards have not yet been set for the breed.

breed. The pedigree certificate is the veri-fied and authenticated proof that a specific cat meets the criteria of the breed. It usual-ly traces back over at least four generations of the animal's ancestry. But the certificate also serves as a guide to breeders in search of exactly the right mix of characteristics.

The process employed by breeders to come up with infant cats that possess desired traits is known as selective breed-ing. Although the science behind the process is incredibly complex, it can be summed up as follows. Every physical fea-ture, and many mental features, of every living thing is controlled by genes. These genes are located on chromosomes, which are paired off in the atomic structure of the animal. When mating results in the union of sperm with egg—also known as fertilisa-tion—the chromosomes of the new being that's just been created are paired. In each pair, half is contributed by the father and half by the mother. These pairings deter-mine the traits of the offspring.

Using these principles, a breeder works to combine just the right parentage to come up with the kittens he desires to produce. The Siamese has probably been refined more through this process than any other breed over the years.

Sometimes—often, as a matter of fact—nature throws a wild card into the process, producing totally unexpected results in the offspring. While only one or two kit-tens in a litter will exhibit a new trait arrived at in this manner, their littermates will be pretty much as anticipated. Mutations such as this often are sterile and

The Somali, resulting from the introduction of long-haired genes into the Abyssinian breed, combines a wild, longhair appearance with the almost delicate body structure of the Oriental breeds.

Although breeders are meeting with a great deal of success in developing new variations in the Somali, the ruddy variation is one of only three currently recognized.

At birth Somali kittens have not yet developed their characteristic colouring and long hair. This develops over the first few months of life.

cannot pass the new trait on to future generations. However, every so often the mutation is also viable and a new characteristic, or even a new breed, can start from that point.

Just as with all traits, expected or not, the new characteristics can be bred for by knowledgeable and patient breeders. Some of the breeds today that have seen their origins in mutation are the American wirehair, Cornish rex, Devon rex, and Sphynx.

Breed and purity of breed, however, are quite relative. Only a small percentage of all cat lovers worldwide actually care at all about the pedigree status of their animals. Only a small percentage of all cats worldwide actually have their papers. The vast majority of cats, of course, are the stray

and feral animals that man's carelessness and lack of concern have created. The next largest proportion of the worldwide cat community is made up of those mixed-breed animals—possibly found at the local animal shelter and brought home—with which the majority of us share our homes and lives.

Tabby or Tom may look pretty much like a show-class Persian, Siamese, or whatever breed, but there's a mix in her or his parentage that precludes pedigree. The experts would pick up on it in an instant. Do we love our cats any less for that 'shortcoming'? Of course not. Most of us never even thought of showing or breeding when we opened our hearts to that little ball of fur.

The Siamese was a much healthier breed prior to an incredible rise in its popularity in the early 1900s, which led to much indiscriminate breeding.

British cat organisations do not officially recognise the white variety of the Turkish Angora, which is a popular variety among American cat fanciers.

The Turkish Angora arose alongside the Persian from the very first long-haired cats introduced into Europe in the sixteenth century. However, the popularity of the Persian eventually outshined the Turkish Angora.

Intelligence

Now, these few years later, we may start to wonder about just who decided to take on whom as a housemate and a friend. Further, most cat owners eventually come to wonder who's in charge. A great many owner-cat relationships appear out of control—at least, out of the owner's control—with the cat making most of the decisions, some of which might coincide with the wishes of the owner.

Such situations, which heap much of the fuel onto the passions of the true cat-haters among the human population, do not need to be the continuing state of affairs. Cats are relatively intelligent animals, on average. Their interest in exploring new places and new circumstances, their general cautiousness, and their ability to solve problems that confront them all give testimony to that intelligence. Until animal intelligence tests are developed, such evidence is the majority of what we have. Nevertheless, even this is fairly convincing.

Another indicator of the cat's thinking abilities comes when it's asleep, in its

As a close relative of the Siamese, the exotic shorthair shares many of that breed's personality traits, including a playful and curious nature.

Exotic shorthairs came into existence as a breed in the 1920s, when European cat organisations excluded the solid-coloured animals from Siamese categories and breeders created the new grouping.

British cat organisations consider each colour type of the Persian as a separate breed. They also use the term longhair to describe them.

The chinchilla Persian was produced by selective crossbreedings to build on the dark-tipped fur qualities that first showed up in litters of Persians in the early 1900s.

Would-be owners of a Persian should plan on frequent, elaborate brushings to maintain the quality of the coat that more than likely attracted them to the breed in the first place.

dreams. Watch a sleeping cat for even a short time—it's easy to find one, as the average cat sleeps anywhere from sixteen to eighteen hours per day—and you'll see plenty of evidence of brain activity.

Researchers have gone a bit further, employing the technology of electroencephalograms (EEGs) to derive graphic representations of cat brain activity. Such testing has distinguished various phases of sleep. During the day, when we might best describe it as 'catnapping', the sleep is light. The cat's muscles are never totally relaxed. The sleep is interrupted regularly.

When the cat remains in light sleep for half an hour or so without waking, its brain will enter deep sleep. This phase, which occurs in many forms of life, is commonly known as rapid eye movement (REM) sleep because that's exactly what is happening. The eyelids are closed, but beneath those flaps of skin the eyes flutter rapidly in brief spurts. REM sleep and light sleep periods alternate irregularly.

In addition to EEG readings of the cat's brain activity, which indicate dreamlike waves, the cat offers a pretty convincing argument of its own for the fact that it does dream. Body position changes frequently. Ears and nose are flicked. Whiskers twitch. Legs, paws, and claws are flexed, relaxed, and flexed again. Sometimes the cat even will utter a few vocalisations.

The first bicolour Persians to be shown were placed in the 'any other colour' category for judging, but as the patterns persisted they won their own breed standards.

Common misconception about the ragdoll holds that members of this breed cannot feel pain because their ancestry traces to a white Persian female injured in a traffic accident. This is simply not true.

When held, a ragdoll generally relaxes its muscles to the point that it hangs limply like the child's toy. It is this trait that inspired its name.

The ragdoll is not an overly common breed outside the United States. It remains controversial and not officially recognised as a breed among many cat organisations.

Following page:

Automotive travel is an enjoyable activity for most Burmese cats, especially if they are given the opportunity to look out through the windows during the trip.

When the cat is awake, it may utter a few of the same vocalisations under certain circumstances. Although they don't have a language on the same level as humans, cats also don't have the same level of complex concepts to communicate. As with most species of higher animals, cats have plenty of language, although not nearly all in the form of vocalisations, to communicate what they are thinking.

Body Language

Body language is the most important component of cat communication, and nearly every part of the body gets into the act.

The tail reveals a great deal about the cat's mood. Twitching from side to side reveals a growing level of excitement and anticipation, while broader strokes that might best be described as waving signify the heightened mood of annoyance. A tail held upright, such as when one cat sniffs the anal region of another cat, is the signature of an open, friendly cat. If the upright tail also twitches a bit, the cat is probably open to interaction but alert for anything potentially threatening. If it decides that it is indeed being threatened or that it should attack, the twitch will change over to a swooshing motion just before it acts on those feelings.

At the same time as the tail goes through its various motions, the legs are sending out some amplifications of their own. A bend in the forelegs signifies an animal that would prefer to avoid a fight but nevertheless is quite willing to defend itself. If the hind legs are bent, the cat is undecided about its

The ideal home for a ragdoll is a tranquil household without many disturbances of any sort, where the cat will enjoy a sense of security and protection.

The purebred Abyssinian carries the stereotypical build of the mummified cats and carved images found in ancient Egyptian tombs.

position but leaning toward timidity. If both legs are bent, you're looking at an uncertain and defensive animal. On the other hand, should the cat stretch its legs to their maximum, it is confident in its relative position and fully ready to attack if warranted.

The head also conveys a lot about the cat's mood. If the cat pushes its head forward, and maybe tilts it a bit, it is seeking some contact. When the cat raises its head erectly, it is trying to display dominance. By contrast, if it lowers its head, it is accepting an inferior, or even submissive, position. And, if it lowers its head so far that the chin actually 'tucks' into the chest, the cat really isn't all that interested in whatever's taking place.

Interest and anticipation are shown with ears slanted forward, while ears pricked back are precursors of attack. If the ears have a sideways slant to them, the cat is fearful, defensive, and prepared to flee. Generally upright ears are the position of contentment.

And, tying it all together, is the emotionally driven body of the animal. A confident or attack-prone cat will stretch its body out as much as possible. However, a fearful or defensive cat will arch its back into the stereotypical Halloween-cat-type position. A special, hunkered-down, exposed posture

Abyssinians are a strong, robust breed that need a great deal of play and regular time outdoors.

In their first few months of life, Abyssinian kittens appear to belong in some other breed category. They generally are covered with dark markings that gradually fade.

Buster Brown was the name of the very first of the American shorthair breed. He looked much like this latter-day version of the breed.

The first ancestors of the American shorthair were the first domestic cats to arrive in America. They came as ship cats on the first voyages to the New World.

Like the European shorthairs from which it originated, the American shorthair began as a semi-tame breed, running the streets and alleys of colonial America.

Give-and-take is key to a relationship with an American shorthair. The breed is almost doglike in its show of affection for the entire family, so long as that affection and respect are returned.

known as lordosis is reserved for the female when she's ready to mate.

An awareness of all these visual signals is a useful tool for anyone wanting to train a cat. Contrary to much popular belief, nearly every cat can be trained. As we've shown, the cat is an intelligent animal. With such intelligence comes the ability to be trained, alongside a high level of independence, which some might interpret as stubbornness, laziness, or even stupidity.

Training Cats

This naturally leads to some comparisons with our other favourite domestic animal, the dog. The cat and the dog seem to occupy much the same niche within our households, so why not consider the qualities of one against the other. The very good reasons for not making such comparisons—except in deciding which animal will best fit into your household—is the simple fact that cats and dogs are very different ani-

The curly hair of the American wirehair is a dominant genetic trait that will surface regularly in breedings with nonwirehair cats.

The ocicat is one of the new designer breeds, which breeders are producing in many new and different patterns to the specifications of anxious owners.

The colourpoint
shorthair enjoys
contact with
people, particularly
those who give
it the kind and
gentle attention
that it craves.

The colourpoint
shorthair is a
developing breed,
with new colours
and patterns
being introduced
regularly through
the breeding of
Siamese cats with
other types.

The Cymric began as a long-haired mutation of the Manx that showed up among litters of the latter in Canada in the 1960s.

mals at their most basic levels.

There are many differences that we could discuss here, but the one that lies at the heart of the matter and actually explains most of the others is this: Cats are solitary animals by nature, born with the instinct to survive on their own, coming into contact with other cats only during special occasions and circumstances. Dogs, by contrast, are pack animals, born with the instinct for group behaviour, action, and survival.

The pack instinct accounts for the dog's eagerness to follow our commands and fulfill our wishes. The animal has transferred its feelings for the pack to its new human pack, usually accepting the various humans in the family in various pack roles from leader to subservient.

Cats have no such instincts to transfer into the human household setting. To train a cat—and it most definitely can be done—we must remember the motivations that rule the animal's life: the 'likes' of food, warmth, and companionship (within limits) and the 'dislikes' of water, cold, and loud noise. Any owner, keeping these factors in mind and combining them with love, patience, and gentleness, can teach a cat at least a few behaviours and tricks.

Most cats, at least those that did not experience deprivation in their kittenhoods, have very active minds that will eagerly welcome and respond to periodic, if not prolonged, training sessions. Those minds need a constant flow of stimulation to maintain the keen, active edges. In studies involving EEG monitoring of cats'

Like its first cousin, the Abyssinian, the Egyptian Mau has the appearance of the first domestic cats that roamed ancient Egyptian thousands of years ago.

A naturally occurring breed in Egypt, the Egyptian Mau first emerged out of Egypt only in the 1950s. 'Mau' derives from the ancient Egyptian word for cat.

All Himalayans are colourpoint cats, with their namesake colours appearing on the points—ears, face, legs, feet, and tails. This is a tortoiseshell-point specimen.

The Japanese bobtail is a unique, naturally occurring breed that developed without introduction of other genetics on the island country from which it draws its name.

The Havana did not originate on the Caribbean island of Cuba, as its name would imply. The British breeders who developed the breed arrived at the name because of its cigar colour.

brains, it has been demonstrated that a lack of stimulus will actually lead to a shutdown of the brain to the minimum level needed for basic survival.

To help to satisfy the need, and for the rewards that we covered earlier, most cats welcome training in short, friendly sessions. A total training session of ten minutes is close to the maximum that should be attempted. However, repeated sessions on the same behaviour will not lessen the cat's interest in the activity.

In such training, the giving of a reward is always the preferred treatment. Unlike dogs, cats will not respond to the withholding of something they want by performing a desired behaviour. They will simply lose interest and go off in search of their own means to gain that reward or some new pursuit.

Similarly, punishment never has the desired impact on a cat in training, even punishment to the extent of a raised voice. To bring undesired behaviour to an end, many cat owners have found an indirect, anonymous approach to bring the quickest and most lasting results. When a cat is scratching the side of a couch, for instance, a small ball of paper lofting across the living room from some unknown source and then lightly bumping the cat on the back of the head will soon force the animal to associate the attack with the behaviour. A small squirt from a water pistol, delivered in similar anonymity, can have the same effect.

Cats, like all living creatures, greatly dislike the unknown, particularly when the unknown seems to be attacking. If the owner is careful in delivering these 'attacks', so that the cat never makes the connection, it will come to associate the negative consequences with the behaviour that the owner wants to bring to an end.

It is especially important to neuter cats allowed to roam outdoors on their own to avoid unwanted litters of kittens.

INSTINCTIVE BEHAVIOUR

The tail of the Japanese bobtail resembles those of some dog breeds whose tails are purposefully chopped when the animals are very young. However, the bobtail in the cat is naturally occurring.

To many cat owners one of the most disturbing behaviours in the cat is its inherent insistence to remain an animal with an ancestry of predators. Even the most well-fed, housebound cat retains at least some of the hunting instinct, as well as a deep-seated need to act on that instinct. The feline biology needs a high level of protein to function and prosper, which explains why attempts to convert cats to vegetarianism have consistently failed.

But this doesn't negate the repulsion that some owners feel when the warm and cuddly bundle of fur that sleeps at the foot of their bed and gently laps milk from a saucer presents them with a freshly killed mouse or songbird. They would feel even stranger about the whole affair if they realized that the action is something of an insult, albeit well intentioned, to them. The cat isn't really presenting this trophy for praise. It's offering the morsel to the owner, who doesn't seem able to kill prey for himself or herself.

The very first member of the Himalayan breed, a cat known as Debutante was born in the unlikely setting of the Harvard Medical College in 1935.

The island of Bali has absolutely no connection with the Balinese breed, although its graceful movements can be reminiscent of the dancers of that island.

As can be seen in these blue-and-white Persians, the word blue is defined rather liberally when applied to cat breeds.

All cats share this hunting instinct. But they vary widely when it comes to acting upon that urge. To a large extent, the hunting ability of a cat is dependent upon the hunting ability of its mother. When she feels that her kittens are mature enough to begin their training, the mother cat will begin bringing live prey back to them. She permits the kittens to play with these injured or stunned victims, learning to use their claws and teeth as they do. As their skills advance, she returns with gradually more lively prey. When the kittens have advanced sufficiently, she begins leading them afield to further develop their skills.

Nearly all kittens advance to the stalk-and-pounce level in their training, but the ability to finish the hunt with a kill seems to be the point that divides the real hunters from those who will dabble with it in a sportlike manner during their adulthood. In other words, nearly all cats can hunt and most can capture prey, but a smaller proportion of the species can pur-

The Balinese breed remains rather rare in Great Britain, although it has been officially recognised in the United States since 1968. It first surfaced as a mutation in a litter of Siamese kittens.

When the Japanese bobtail sits, it often raises its front paw, which according to island lore is a precursor of good fortune settling on the home where the animal lives.

61

The most likely explanation for the origins of the Birman places the cats in the position of near-deities in the Buddhist temples of Burma.

posefully and regularly make the kill. A primary factor in this division of ability levels lies with the abilities that the mother possessed to pass along to her kittens and the circumstances under which she was able to train them.

Even the best mousers don't kill everything they pursue. Observations of such cats in factories have found that almost half of all mice escape the feline clutches.

However, if the unnatural repulsion that some of us feel when anything dies—even when that death comes as a result of very natural instincts and actions—can be put aside, a skilled cat on the hunt is truly a thing of beauty. The feline positions itself very carefully in ambush near the opening where it expects to spot its prey. Its patience in waiting in that position for a considerable amount of time is a lesson from which we humans could benefit. When the prey is spotted, the cat tenses its muscles and launches itself into an arch pounce, landing directly upon the mouse, bird, or other animal with its front paws. Its rear paws alight softly behind it.

In a cat with the ability to kill, the end comes swiftly for the captured prey, through a quick bite at the base of the neck. Such a bite severs the spinal cord, resulting in near-instant death. On the other hand, if the cat lacks the killing ability or isn't really hunting, it may begin to 'play' with the prey creature, tossing it into the air and recapturing it again.

The inherent dislike, or even fear, of the unknown in cats discussed earlier lies at the heart of a very common misconception about the animals. Many well-intentioned cat fanciers, perhaps wanting the cat to be more than the animal it is, will explain quite earnestly how cats insist on going off on their own to die alone. Some will even cite case histories of cats they've personally known who have done exactly that. The cats in these tales exhibit seemingly mystic abilities to sense what's coming and to take the necessary precautions to 'end it all' on their own terms. All this is very much akin to the legendary elephant graveyards of Africa and, just as those bits of lore, the cat-death scenario has a natural explanation.

Females of the Birman breed are eager breeders that must be constantly monitored and restrained to prevent unwanted litters of kittens from those that have not been neutered.

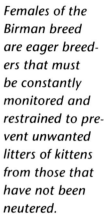

The black coat of the Bombay is responsible for the name of this breed. To the breeders that developed the breed by crossing Burmese and American shorthairs, their results resembled the black leopard of India.

The British short-hair is a naturally occurring breed refined from the street cat of Great Britain over the past century or so.

The British shorthair has retained the look of the street cat in its stocky and muscular body as well as the disposition of that type of animal in a friendly and affectionate attitude.

There is no scientific evidence to support the idea that cats possess some special powers to accomplish such feats. To the contrary, everything we know as fact tells us that the cats do not have a concept of death. What they do have a concept of, however, is pain and suffering, illness and injury. And, cats react to these "attacks" from unknown and unseen enemies in the only way they know how. They try to hide from the enemy. Unfortunately, the enemy travels right along with them, right into their favourite and most secure hiding places, driving them farther and farther into what they hope will be more secure locations.

Comfort and security are two primary motivations in the life of nearly every cat. Much of what the animal does every day is done with those two factors in mind. It is these two factors that play a very high priority in the cat's establishment of its territory.

Cats are by nature very territorial. They are most comfortable and secure when

Although the Tonkinese makes a near-perfect household pet, it also relishes excursions into the outdoors.

The Tonkinese is one of the most affectionate breeds. It craves a return of that attitude from all members of the household.

they have regular, self-assigned spots for each of their regular activities: eating, sleeping, socialising, relieving themselves, and so on. Even a one hundred percent in-the-house cat, which has never set foot beyond the door step, has its territory, albeit an indoor domain.

Memory and the Senses

A cat's territory remains a very essential part of the animal's memory. 'Memory?' some of you may ask, thinking of the times you tried to teach a cat a lasting lesson, such as not to scratch the furniture or not to climb to the top shelf of the entertainment center in the living room. Your experience may have led you to the very definite conclusion that cats in general have rather short memories. But then, how do we explain the abilities they demonstrate regularly to remember where they prefer to hoard their favourite toys or the best spots in their territories for stalking prey?

The fact is that cats do have very good memories, for things they feel are important to them. As with just about everything else about the cat, its memory is reserved for its own self-centred purposes. This is a critical concept for anyone wanting to teach something to a cat. Think like a cat, keep the central motivations of the cat in mind, and relate whatever it is you're trying to teach to one or more of those motivations. Further, remember that motivations for a cat are just as likely to be 'likes' as 'dislikes'.

Cats further demonstrate their rather strong memories in their seemingly

The Burmese has one of the longest potential lifespans of all the domestic cat breeds. Members of the breed have been documented as old as age eighteen.

The blue British shorthair is virtually identical to the Charteaux of France. In fact, the two are generally placed into the same judging categories at cat shows.

A crossing of Siamese and Burmese resulted in the first Tonkinese in the mid-1970s in Canada. It was the first pedigree breed to originate there.

memories surface regularly. Usually these cats have demonstrated a memory for their homes after being transported incredible distances. The media have a real talent for assigning motives of love or longing for their human families to those cats.

While the cat may indeed have special reasons for returning—generally for reasons of comfort or security—it's not the people, but the place, it remembers. If the people had moved while the cat was away, it would still return to the place rather than seek them out.

But it's more than simple memory of its home that allows the cat to perform this feat. An internal biological clock and an extraordinary sense for the earth's magnetic fields are critical to this ability. The cat combines all these 'readings' to fix an angle on the sun in relation to its territory. It then follows that angle home. However, this is not the sure thing that some believe it to be. Actually it appears that the cat engages in quite a bit of trial and error to make this system eventually work.

Further there is some pretty strong evidence that the magnetic fields play a major role in all of this. In experiments where

instant recall of the most minute details in our daily schedules. Almost before the picture tube in the television set has fully dimmed, the cat has nestled into the comforter on the bed, knowing that it's time for sleep. Similarly, Kitty's almost always waiting at the front door when you arrive home from work, then, a couple of hours later, she's there at your feet the instant the can opener begins its whine.

Reports of cats with truly extraordinary

Although Oriental shorthairs crave as much meat in the diet as they can find, an exclusively meat menu tends to dull and otherwise alter the colours of the cat's coat.

magnets have been attached to cats, their orientating and manoeuvreing abilities have been impaired.

That connection to the magnetic fields is just part of the very powerful sensory system with which our domestic cat is equipped. While all of the cat's senses are stronger than ours—for example, the cat can hear sounds about three-and-a-quarter times higher than most humans can detect—it's the link between the senses of smell and taste that is most remarkable.

So intense is this connection that the cat can smell with its tongue and pull scents out of the air with its tongue. At the heart of this mechanism is an extra organ, known as the Jacobson's organ, in the roof of the mouth. Like many other carnivores, the cat seems to curl its upper lip and wrinkle its nose in an action that brings the chemicals of scents into contact with this organ. The Jacobson's organ in turn transfers information about the scents to the hypothalamic region of the cat's brain. Scent information captured in this manner can relate both to appetite and sexual behaviour.

The Burmese is a very old breed. It is described in a book of poems from Thailand that dates back to 1350.

This white Persian kitten will grow into a relatively stocky longhair.

The name of the Korat translates roughly into 'good fortune', and in its home-land of Thailand it is a folk trad-ition to give each new bride a pair of the cats.

Although the Korat is a very curious animal that insists on being familiar with everything in its environment, it is not well adapted to the outside world, where the noises and distrac-tions cause it dis-tress very quickly.

The Korat is not a common breed, even in the Korat province of Thailand, where it originated thousands of years ago.

Farm cats without pedigree and ship cats of the Angora breed were the original ancestors of the Maine coon in the American state of the same name.

The cat's sense of sight is similarly developed to meet the special needs of being a cat. To begin with, its vision is nearly perfect in daylight. The only exception to this is an object just a short distance directly in front of the animal's face. This minor flaw comes about because the cat has the typical predator design to its face. With the eyes set squarely in the front of its head—compare this to the location of a rabbit's eyes—each eye has a range of vision greater than 280 degrees. However, this leaves a slight cone of poor vision directly in front of the animal's nose.

Its vision is only a bit less perfect in the dark. Although the cat cannot see in complete darkness, even the slightest sliver of moonlight or bit of porch light provide enough illumination for the animal to function. The cat's eyes are able to magnify whatever light is available by forty to fifty times. This is accommodated by something called the *tapetum lucidum*, which is an internal cellular lining in each eye that acts like a mirror to reflect light on the retina.

Although the Persian has come to be associated with refined lifestyles, members of the breed in general are good mousers that enjoy playing outdoors.

SPECIAL CONSIDERATIONS

The space available in this book has permitted us only this brief look at the most outstanding aspects of cat physiology, and we are fully aware that this is not a book about cat health and care. However, there are two points that we feel must be made in every cat book that purports to carry a caring message about the animals. These two points are declawing and neutering, and the proper approach to them is don't and do.

In many parts of the world, including the United Kingdom, the declawing procedure is simply illegal. Veterinarians are not permitted to perform the operation.

Unfortunately, declawing remains a relatively common procedure in the United States.

The reason for declawing is nearly always the same: Rather than dealing with problems of scratching with patience and the techniques we described earlier, these owners opt for the simpler and quicker surgical solution. They view declawing as little more than removing a toenail. But, if they were to see this in its true light and put it into human perspective, it would be akin to removing something much more vital, such as our hands.

The cat relies on its claws for a great deal of its agility and manoeuvrability. Removing the claws ultimately removes

With one of the heaviest coats of all domestic cat breeds, the Norwegian forest cat thrives best in a household where temperatures are not kept too high and outdoor time is permitted.

Folklore holds that the Maine coon resulted from the mating of a wild raccoon with a domestic cat. The tale is untrue and genetically impossible.

Breeders of the Manx have carefully guarded the breed against the introduction of any outside influences that could jeopardize the trademark tail-less quality.

Kittens of the Maine coon are very slow to develop. Most don't reach full maturity until their fourth year.

The Norwegian forest cat is a naturally occurring breed that has been recognised by man for thousands of years. It is often mentioned in Nordic legend.

most of the animal's ability to move vertically, and for the cat that ventures outside at all, declawing removes its primary means of both defence and escape.

On the other hand, unless you are planning to breed the cat and can realistically guarantee that no unwanted litters of unwanted kittens will result, neutering is the one medical alteration to the animal that really is an act of kindness and caring. Our streets are already overcrowded with homeless, stray, and feral cats producing new generations of themselves in great profusion. Without very meticulous and constant monitoring and restrictions, every non-neutered cat is a very real potential addition to this problem.

In this light, we can see that neutering is actually an act of love, both for the individual and for the cat population as a whole.

And that's what we've really been saying throughout this book. Accepted on its terms for what it is, and provided with its basic needs (physical and emotional), the cat will contribute its full share to a wonderful relationship with the humans with whom it spends its life.

Both sexes in the Egyptian Mau are willing and eager parents, lavishing care on their kittens and engaging in long periods of play with the young cats.

Most domestic cats sleep sixteen to eighteen hours every day, depending upon their environment and activities taking place around them.

PHOTO CREDITS